HAPPY
BIRTHDAY!

from: La Grande Boucherie!

Written by Jenny Dorsey

Photographed by Melissa Hom

Illustrationns by Anna Lekanidis

Edited by Anya Tchoupakov

Designed by Savvy Studio

Produced by Tijana Masic

3rd edition of 50,000 copies

ISBN 978-0-578-88384-7

Emil Stefkov
Founder and Concept Creator

LA GRANDE BOUCHERIE

Introduction		5
I	La Grande Boucherie	13
	About La Grande Boucherie	14
	The Design of La Grande Boucherie	20
	The Chefs of La Grande Boucherie	30
II	Boucherie Meat	35
	Philosophy for Meat	36
	The Dry Aging Process	40
	Meat Cookery and Presentation	44
III	Boucherie Classics	55
	Classic French Dishes	56
	The Raw Bar	66
	Charcuterie and Cheese	70
	Wine and Cocktails	76

INTRODUCTION

The concept of a boucherie, or "butcher shop" in French, dates back centuries and offers a fascinating glimpse into the historical evolution of France.

From Classical Antiquity (between the 6th and 8th centuries A.D.) up until the French Revolution (1789–1799), the profession of a butcher in France was reserved for a privileged few serving the upper class. Although the nobility only made up of 20% of the total population, urban cities like Paris were consuming shockingly high amounts of meat: 60–80 kilograms (132–176 pounds) per person per year.

Butchers worked together to monitor the market, ensure proper safety procedures, and limit the number of master butchers qualified to sell fresh meat. In Paris during the Middle Ages, each stage of the meat production process — from slaughter to final cuts — took place in a single three-story building known as "la grande boucherie" (the big butcher shop).

Today, boucheries in France are well-loved symbols of the neighborhood. They are spaces of appreciation and education between farmer, artisan, and eater; a reminder of past eras in France where the entirety of one segment of the food system flourished under one roof.

© Laure Albin Guillot / Roger-Viollet

The first Boucherie locations in New York
City were odes to the proud lineage of French
butcher shops, following in their footsteps
of a thoughtful process of doing everything
in-house at the highest quality possible. Over
the last decade, these Boucherie locations
have become places for neighbors to gather,
where friendships begin, romances spark,
and families reunite.

The cultivation of that ever vibrant joie
de vivre, "joy of living," has been the
ultimate centerpiece of Boucherie since the
beginning. Now, as the company ushers in
a new era with the opening of La Grande
Boucherie in Midtown, New York — the
biggest restaurant in the city — the farm-to-
table process encapsulating transparency and
dedication to the French way of life comes
full circle across the Atlantic.

LA GRANDE BOUCHERIE

ABOUT
LA GRANDE
BOUCHERIE

The opening of La Grande Boucherie marks the beginning of a new chapter for the whole Boucherie group. New York's Boucherie restaurants have always operated at the intersection of an indulgent steak house and a refined Parisian brasserie: a place where a diner can feel spoiled and taken care of, at ease enough to relax for a few hours and sip an aperitif while enjoying the sidewalk scene. Now, La Grande Boucherie brings the entirety of that signature French dining scene — the chatty passersby on the street, the colorful tunes of live musicians, the relaxing clink-clink of glassware, the smell of fresh bread — under one roof.

At 12,000 square feet — four times the size of the first Boucherie restaurant — La Grande Boucherie acts as a town square of its Midtown neighborhood. It is situated at the center of a pedestrian gallery at 6 ½ avenue, spanning the entire block between 53rd and 54th street. This is a restaurant that breathes with its adjacent space: the restaurant and the gallery flow effortlessly into one another, the French doors are always open, and the seating merges naturally across the typical boundary between restaurant and sidewalk. Warm globe lights adorn the entirety of the walkway, marking a complete change of environment from "out there" to "in here." For anyone passing through, the energy of the bar is palpable, the glimmer of ice from the raw bar sparklingly visible, the breezy sound of jazz classics from the baby grand piano beckoning them to walk a little slower and enjoy the scene.

The idea is to give the thousands of New Yorkers and visitors crossing through the neighborhood every month a glimpse into the liveliness of a public plaza in France, a place where the people of the neighborhood come to gather, where life happens.

The bright and airy gallery is heated to a temperate 75°F year-round, with 25-foot chandeliers hanging 40 feet above the ground, glimmering alongside the natural light streaming in through the windows. Inside, La Grande Boucherie holds almost 500 seats, so the atmosphere is always dynamic and interactive: everyone is welcome, and no one feels alone. It is a forum where people go out to not only eat but also meet new people, to see how the world is unfolding around them. It is a village in and of itself.

THE DESIGN OF LA GRANDE BOUCHERIE

La Grande Boucherie blends the feeling
of Paris while still grounding guests in
the vivacious nature of New York City, in
a design and concept envisioned by the
founder Emil Stefkov. Intricate details bring
elements of the past into a distinctively
modern space, starting with the doorway
entrance: a set of quadruple French doors
with stained glass, wood cladding, and
ornaments, freshly updated with decorative
metal and hardware. Its façade bridges
tradition with innovation while its slide-and-
push functionality effortlessly joins interior
and exterior.

The first feeling upon stepping into the restaurant is one of grandeur. With 150-year-old glass ceilings 20 feet high and stunning carved wood panels reminiscent of Alexandre Charpentier, guests are transported to a place of fantasy, straddling the rustic world of France's countryside, the extravagance of the belle époque, and the contemporary nature of 21st-century New York City.

Rather than rehashing the motifs already associated with brasseries, the design elements of La Grande Boucherie "belong more to our time," describes co-designer Julien Legeard. This extends to everything in the space, from plaster work and painting to metal and wood: "We use executions that respect the tradition of these art forms," says Julien.

The flow and rhythm of the space is beguiling and effortless. Every architectural element is in sync with one another, from the Art Nouveau balcony (styled after the iconic Samaritaine in Paris) to the thoughtful metalwork of the railings, balconies, and awnings by Sylvain Mabille de Poncheville.

The ceiling curves from room to room are complex lunette curves inspired by the famous Brasserie Excelsior in Nancy, while the nostalgic tiled floors are brightened with hues of yellow and red inspired by the work of Victor Horta. Two mezzanines overlook the restaurant, offering guests a closer view of the ceiling and stained-glass façade, and smooth columns embellished with warm round lights offer transitions between each section of the ground floor.

La Grande Boucherie is very different from its siblings, yet it maintains important threads of consistency. The seating is one such area of commonality, with circular tables and the familiar woven chairs made of brown and burgundy leather. The kitchen brings in elements of the original Boucherie restaurants as well, with subway tiles and the natural mix-and-match of artwork with equipment.

Not to be overlooked, the bathrooms were treated as one of the most important aspects of the space: the floors are blended with custom marble, and the ceilings are detailed with plaster decor and gold-leaf effects, finished with intricate wood ornaments.

The statement piece of the restaurant, as in every Boucherie, is the bar. Its counter was handmade made with 200 year old molds and techique at L'Etainier Tourangeau in France, forged from pewter — the traditional material for bars — custom edges and border decals. The lower portion of the bar integrates wood ornaments with aged gold leafing, giving off a sense of understated glamor.

Together, the architectural elements of La Grande Boucherie play into the foundational essence of Art Nouveau: organic lines and patterns inspired by nature, a feeling of movement throughout a space that links structure with fine arts.

Given La Grande Boucherie's proximity
to much of New York's cultural scene —
Broadway, Central Park, MoMA — it acts as
a fitting retreat for those seeking an indulgent
getaway that still feels close to home.

THE CHEFS OF LA GRANDE BOUCHERIE

La Grande Boucherie has expanded the Boucherie family in new and wonderful ways. While some of the team have been with us for years, others are just joining us to bring fresh ideas to the company. Having seen just about everything in the industry — including, now, a worldwide pandemic — we are sticking together as a family, supporting each other and looking forward toward a shared future.

CHEF BILL BRASILE
Culinary Strategy and Development

Chef Bill brings a deep-seated passion for French cuisine and culture, expertise in whole-animal butchery and charcuterie, and years of experience at some of the most notable pioneering restaurants in the US and Europe.

Chef Bill began cooking professionally in the mid-90s in Washington, DC, under Richard Poye, former Chef de Cuisine for Nora Pouillon, a pioneer of organic cuisine in the US. After attending the Culinary Institute of America, Chef Bill arrived in New York City in 1998 and has since worked in some of New York City's most iconic restaurants, such as Le Cirque, Wallsé, Lespinasse, Morimoto, Minetta Tavern, and Frenchette.

In 2008, Bill was about to open a bistro in Paris, but he returned to New York as part of the opening team at Minetta Tavern, where he served as Chef de Cuisine for four years, then as Executive Chef for three more. Minetta Tavern has earned a Michelin star every year since 2010, as well as a three-star review from The New York Times.

After departing Minetta Tavern in 2016, Bill joined the staff of NYU as an adjunct professor for Hospitality Operations, and he consulted on openings for several restaurants in New York, including James Beard award-winner Frenchette, 10 Corso Como, Pier 17 at the South Street Seaport for Howard Hughes, and Little Frog Bistro. He joined the Boucherie family to open La Grande Boucherie in 2020.

DOMINICK PEPE
Corporate Executive Chef

One of Chef Dominick's earliest memories is spending hours watching his Italian grandmother carefully preparing fresh pasta. He was mesmerized by the dedication and love she put into every family meal. He later translated that passion into a degree in hospitality, and while working at a family restaurant in Florida, it became clear that he wanted to pursue the life of a chef.

After moving to New York City in 2012 to take a sous chef position at Italian trattoria Olio e Piú, he quickly rose to Executive Chef of the restaurant.

In 2015, he opened Dominique Bistro, building the menu and kitchen from the ground up, bringing to life his true vision for the intimate French bistro. In 2016, Chef Dominick worked with Chef Jerome Dihui from Pastis to build the menu for Boucherie.

Chef Dominick prefers a classic approach to food, yet is also inspired by new ingredients and plating styles. With a passion for information and an insatiable reading habit, he is constantly expanding his culinary perspective, always striving to provide happiness for those who eat at his restaurants.

BOUCHERIE
MEAT

PHILOSOPHY FOR MEAT

Thoughtful integration at every step of the supply chain is at the heart of Boucherie's meat program. The meats of La Grande Boucherie are carefully chosen from single-family or boutique farmers following a permaculture mindset for creating resilient ecosystems on their land, using regenerative agriculture to promote both healthier crops and happy animals. "These are animals not raised on a large scale. They are eating the foods of the farm — not feed purchased from outside vendors — and grazing on pasture with a variety of flowers and grass," Chef Bill explains. This way, even the meat offers a sense of terroir, in addition to being slightly leaner, with a more mineral finish.

Given the holistic nature of the Boucherie programs, Chef Bill works closely with farmers to adjust aspects of the cow's life cycle so the eventual product is aligned with his vision. A major part of this process is adjusting the "finishing," or the last few months of the cow's diet, so it is suitable for its eventual preparation. In many high-volume production ranches, cows will be moved off their natural surroundings to a new place where they are fattened on corn before slaughter, thereby accentuating the fattiness and marbling in their meat. Chef Bill takes an active stance against this: "I want to taste the actual breed of the animal without the over-the-top finishing," he explains, "otherwise, it's hard to distinguish its characteristics or the location where it grew up."

Location is such an important aspect to Chef Bill because it influences flavor far more than many consumers are aware. "Take a higher altitude cow, like a Swiss cow," Chef Bill gives as an example. "It has a pristine white fat that's very thick and very pure — it's noticeable if you've tasted it, and the notes of the grass and its feed come through very clearly." Within the US, a Midwestern cow will taste different than one raised in Vermont due to the regional differences in climate, wild grass, elevation, seasons, and more. By emphasizing the importance of birthplace and the roaming habits of the cow, the final meats coming out of La Grande Boucherie's kitchen are consistently superior to the beef handled through a commercial feed lot.

No matter the farmer, breed, or location, Chef Bill personally samples the beef to ensure it's up to par. To evaluate, he slices off a small sliver, adds a touch a sea salt, and eats it raw. "I'm looking for tactile cues before I even taste it," he says, "I rub my hands over the fat to feel if it is waxy, porous, moist — that tells me a lot about the breeding and feeding process." The fat on Wagyu cows, for example, is soapy and waxy, almost like "rubbing jade," while most American cows have a drier, harder fat. "I always make sure to examine the bigger joints of the animal, so I can see how it's been treated," he continues, "I want to see that the bones are strong, how well developed certain areas are, what type of structure the whole animal has."

The contrast between which body parts
have lean versus higher-muscular fat is also
important in determining the final use of those
cuts. "There's a lot of the animal that's ground
up, or used for braising," Chef Bill explains,
"but not all braising cuts are made equal —
some, like the paleron cut (chuck) from the
shoulder will stay moist in a long cook while
a shank often dries out. It's important to cook
them for different amounts of time for the best
final product."

THE DRY AGING PROCESS

Given the large scope of La Grande Boucherie's meat program, it makes sense to use as much of the whole animal as possible. Whereas the former Boucherie locations were too small to accommodate full carcasses, Chef Bill has made it a point to bring the carving and aging process in-house. "It's just like aging a whole wheel of cheese," he says, "it's a totally different end result of the meat when we can dry age a whole animal to our own specifications."

By aging the largest piece of meat possible, the beef will lose less moisture over time and develop more complex layers of flavor across all its cuts. "We're adding more lifespan to the beef by doing it this way," Chef Bill explains. "By aging the whole carcass to condition this 'baseline' of quality, we can then further age smaller cuts — such as a côte de boeuf (rib steak) — for an extended amount of time without compromising moisture or texture." A côte de boeuf from La Grande Boucherie could feasibly be aged 90 days in total while "retaining fresher flavors and moisture levels" compared to those from other restaurants, who would typically max out at 45 days.

By developing the dry aging program from scratch, Chef Bill has been able to pinpoint when the optimum times are for each section of beef — which varies by cow — and control every piece of the puzzle from temperature and humidity to hang time. "The larger the cut, the slower it goes," he explains. The whole animal will hang and dry age for 28 to 36 days before the team breaks it down into primal sides. These sections are further analyzed and aged to develop the flavors necessary for its final presentation. "This way, we're able to serve cuts that are usually not able to be dry aged before serving," Chef Bill continues. "Cuts like hanger steak, rump steak, top sirloin, bar steak — these are not attached to a bone and typically will dry out." These cuts are usually taken from the dry aged carcass and cooked straight from there, because "leaner cuts don't take to dry aging as well as bone-in or fattier cuts." However, aging the whole cow still gives the team time to imbue some complexity into these pieces.

Bone-in cuts, on the other hand, are split from the whole carcass and aged further. "Just like hanging game birds or cheese, meat tenderizes over time and the flavors concentrate," Chef Bill explains. "We're looking for controlled decomposition and continued intensification of flavor." This way, the beef is always optimized to its best possible state before making its final journey to the guest's plate.

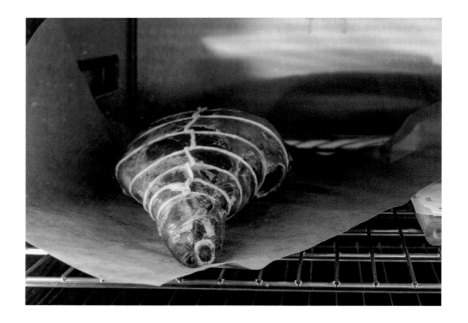

MEAT COOKERY AND PRESENTATION

There is a plan for each and every cut of beef at La Grande Boucherie. Muscles that are not used as frequently on the cow — often from the back or the belly — are naturally more tender, so Chef Bill keeps these as the option to be cooked medium-rare to medium. Filet mignon is the poster child of this category, and while other cuts like top sirloin may not be as meltingly tender, they still offer a lovely texture.

But "tenderness isn't everything," Chef Bill says. "Take the flatiron cut. You have to do some work to it since it has tendons and the like, but it has an incredible amount of flavor." In fact, many of the classic French cuts, such as flatiron, côte de boeuf, or rump steak, emphasize higher intramuscular fat and fuller flavor. These are often called "butcher's pieces" because they are the small, unique cuts that a butcher would keep for themselves. From the spider steak (araignée) and pear steak (poire) to the hanger steak (onglet) and skirt steak (hampe), these may be new to the American palate despite their long tradition in France.

For those who may be skeptical, Chef Bill explains that "aging also helps a lot in tenderizing these cuts. We hang them for 28 days before the individual steaks are broken off." Adding some time for marinating — in olive oil or wine — also adds some interesting depth. The entrecôte (ribeye), for example, is a cut that's sliced very thin, marinated in olive oil and herbs, and grilled very quickly over high heat and served rare.

The hefty intramuscular fat structure of tender cuts is also a prized part of tougher braising and grinding cuts, typically from the shoulders or legs of the animal. The bigger cuts end up in dishes like our signature boeuf bourguignon (Chef Bill likes to use the shoulder or chuck for that) or beef pot-au-feu (typically a mix of shank, short ribs, and marrow), while scraps are used to flavor other dishes like French onion soup (which is made with beef stock).

46

Much like his philosophy with sourcing and aging, Chef Bill's outlook on presentation is focused on highlighting the ingredient without letting other things get in the way. "I like to keep things simple and straightforward," he says. "Not too many garnishes, nothing unnecessary. We are not composing dishes with beef as an ingredient, beef is the ingredient." As such, steaks usually don't come adorned with too much besides the classics: salad, frites, roast potatoes. "I'm concerned about how the food is going to eat best, not how it looks," he explains, "like the slice-and-fan method — you lose a lot of juice that way, so we don't do it unless we have good reason."

Similarly, the sauces served alongside each cut are always thoughtful: bordelaise, rich and meaty with red wine and bone marrow; au poivre, spicy and creamy with coarse peppercorns; veal peppercorn, juicy and decadent with a touch of brandy or cognac. These can be roughly categorized under three umbrellas: an emulsion of either hot or cold ingredients (such as vinaigrettes and aiolis); a thickened sauce using a roux (such as bechamel); and the deglazed sauces made during the process of cooking meats.

La Grande Boucherie's house sauce is a bearnaise, a derivation of the famed hollandaise with a splash of vinegar. "I put a little mustard in there, too," Chef Bill shares with a grin, "It's an expensive sauce, no doubt — we're getting in some really good farm eggs and butter. I want it to taste like it does in France: rich, in your face, with a thick and shiny consistency." He likens it to a French hot sauce with the addition of mustard: "for the people who want just a little bit of spice."

Even the pepper in the pepper mills — tall, wooden and graceful — helps bring out the best of the beef. "I wanted a bridge between fresh, strong, and straightforward black pepper with something more aromatic," explains Chef Bill. The question "Would you like some freshly ground pepper?" is something diners have heard dozens of times before, but at La Grande Boucherie, an extra level of service has already been thought of and incorporated into this simple act. "We have really good mills, and all different types of black pepper," says Chef Bill, "kampot noir, kampot rouge, tellicherry, malabar, wild peppercorns from Nepal and Madagascar. It just makes for something really special."

DAUBE DE BOEUF PROVENÇALE

Beef Stew with Red Wine and Carrots.
Wine pairing recommendation: Château Brillette, Moulis en Médoc, Bordeaux, 2017

INGREDIENTS *Serves 2*

500g beef chuck steak
200ml red wine
80g fennel, diced
1 onion, diced
80g of carrot, chopped diagonally
4 garlic cloves, chopped small
2g fresh thyme
2g fresh rosemary
4g fresh parsley
1g fresh sage
1.5g black pepper
Sea salt, to taste
25g vegetable oil
25g olive oil
5g tomato paste
0.5g paprika, sweet
1 orange peel, julienned
1g herbes de provence, dried
50g fresh tomatoes, peeled, seeded, and diced
60g Niçoise olives
1g lavender, dried
40 tomato confit, petals 4 pieces
200g coquillettes pasta, cooked

PREPARATION

1. Trim the excess fat and silver skin from the beef.

2. Cube the beef into 50-gram square pieces, and marinate in red wine, fennel, onion, carrot, garlic, and herbs for a night.

3. Remove beef from marinade, discard vegetables and herbs, then strain the marinade through a small-hole strainer. Reduce marinade by two-thirds, skim the white foam, then strain again and reserve the liquid. Season beef with salt and pepper.

4. Heat vegetable oil in a large casserole, and sear the beef in batches until each piece is browned. Pour off the cooking oil.

5. In the same casserole, turn heat to medium, and add olive oil, onions, and garlic, and cook until translucent and sweet. Add tomato paste and fry lightly for 1–2 minutes, then turn off the heat and add paprika, orange peel, herbes de provence, fresh herbs, and tomatoes.

6. Deglaze with red wine marinade and cook until reduced again by half, stirring lightly to keep it from sticking. Add the beef and resting juices to the pot, then add fresh red wine, olives, and fennel. Simmer and cook covered in an oven for 2.5 hours or until beef is tender. Add dried lavender and tomato confit petals and stir.

7. Let rest for at least one hour before cooling and storing for 1–2 nights in the refrigerator. Reheat and serve with chopped parsley, lavender, and coquillette pasta.

BOUCHERIE CLASSICS

CLASSIC FRENCH DISHES

There are some dishes that have been, and always will be, on the Boucherie menu: French onion soup, boeuf bourguignon, escargots, bouillabaisse, steak frites, among others. "This is where we must put our best foot forward," Chef Bill says, almost solemnly. "These are the dishes everyone is judged by, the classic everyone knows and has a good idea of what they should taste like."

With a bigger space and kitchen team, La Grande Boucherie also offers French classics that are rarely seen on American menus: items like joue de boeuf braisé (beef cheek), pied de porc farci (stuffed pig's feet), even galette sarrasin à la saucisse (Breton crepe with sausage). Chef Bill is thrilled at the prospect of introducing some of these favorites to a new audience: "There's so much of French cuisine that's still untapped here in New York."

He likens some of these classics to songs: "If someone sings I Remember April, they are standing up against giants. It's very different if we just invent something, since people can't really judge." As such, he is determined to make La Grande Boucherie the reference point for these dishes in the US.

"I want to spoil our customers for the next 10 years from eating it anywhere else," he says with a chuckle. "I want them to have the idea in their head that 'It's just not as good as at La Grande Boucherie.'"

His plan to do so is all about kitchen execution and timing. Every plate has its own living force in the kitchen, and it needs to be prepared fresh and brought quickly to the table. "It's important to jump on something when it still has that life in it," Chef Bill explains. "You can't do that when you prepare it in advance and it's stored in, then out, of a fridge. I make sure to leave the fresh preparations to the last minute." Following this thought has come the roast beef cart, which is wheeled around the dining room offering fresh slices to guests. "It's all about making this experience extra memorable."

SOUPE À L'OIGNON GRATINÉE

Classic French onion soup.
Wine pairing recommendation: Pinot Gris from Alsace.

INGREDIENTS   *Serves 1*

½ cup neutral oil
10 large Spanish onions, peeled and sliced
12 large garlic cloves, thinly sliced
1oz fresh thyme, chopped
1qt white wine
1qt veal stock
8qts beef stock
Kosher salt, to taste
Ground black pepper, to taste
2oz sherry vinegar

GARNISH
Gruyere, grated
Crostini, toasted

PREPARATION

1. Place a large pot (rondeau) on medium heat, and add oil.

2. Add the onions, stirring continuously until they are translucent (approximately 1 hour).

3. Once translucent, keep stirring as the onions start to caramelize.

4. Once onions reach a dark brown color, add the garlic and thyme.

5. Cook for 2 more minutes and deglaze with the wine, cooking until the wine has evaporated (approximately 2 minutes).

6. Add the rest of the liquids and bring to a boil.

7. Reduce heat and let simmer for 30 minutes over very low flame, constantly stirring.

8. Season with salt, pepper, and sherry vinegar at the end.

9. Add croutons into the soup and cover with Gruyere. Cook in broiler until cheese is melted and golden.

PÂTÉ DE CAMPAGNE

Country Pâté.
Wine pairing recommendation: Gewurztraminer, Pierre Sparr, Alsace

INGREDIENTS   *Serves 2*

1.5lb pork belly
1lb pork jowl
1.5lb pork shoulder
1lb pork or chicken liver
25ml white wine
25ml cognac
175ml milk
100g onions
7.5g garlic
150g egg
37.5g Kosher salt
1 whole nutmeg
3g quatre épices
50g parsley, chopped
50g lardo or bacon, diced
50g pistachios, roughly chopped

MIREPOIX

12.5g carrot
12.5g celery
12.5g garlic
2 sprigs of parsley
2 sprigs of thyme
12.5g white mushrooms
12.5g shallots

Caul fat, as needed

PREPARATION

1. Season all meat with salt, white wine, and cognac overnight or for up to 3 days.

2. Grind all meat (except the liver) with grinder set on ¼" die plate.

3. Puree liver in blender until smooth.

4. Simmer milk with mirepoix for 20 minutes, then rest, covered, for 45 minutes to infuse. Strain.

5. In a large mixing bowl, combine all ingredients and mix in a large mixer or by hand. (Separate into multiple batches if necessary.)

6. Preheat oven to 325°F.

7. Line terrine molds with caul fat.

8. Fill terrine molds with meat mixture, and wrap tops with caul fat.

9. Season tops of terrines with black pepper, quatre épices, and Espelette pepper.

10. Bake in a bain-marie at 325°F until internal temperature is 158°F.

11. Rest terrines until cooled to room temperature, then place in the refrigerator for up to 3 days before serving.

THE RAW BAR

New York City is a town that loves steaks and shellfish, and La Grande Boucherie is staying true to that tradition. "It's a classic thing," Chef Bill says, "and it has sound business sense, too. If someone comes in and sees fresh, pristine seafood and shellfish over glistening ice, it says something about the values of that restaurant." This is certainly the case even with the prevalence of health inspections: "We're showing our customers how serious we are about preserving freshness in all of our products."

This visual reassurance of quality isn't found only in New York City. "Look at the carts for desserts, the French cheese carts," Chef Bill continues. "They get the customers' mouths watering, excited for the next course."

The raw bar also functions as the perfect way to ease diners into a relaxed meal. "Setting the stage for the first course is huge in a steakhouse," Chef Bill explains. "It gives a chance for some of our really lovely white wines to be showcased and immediately slows down the pace of the dining room so guests can unwind." It also offers some satiation before the main meats arrive, with the light brininess of the seafood helping to whet appetites. "It's just enough to make people excited, something else to start a meal with raw and living things."

To Chef Bill, attention to detail is everything in the raw bar — from the oysters on display to the lemons quartered alongside them. The mignonette is delicate but flavorful, with freshly ground butter and sliced shallots. There is no room for bagged oyster crackers here: "The bread we're serving with our seafood is a traditional sourdough rye with fresh butter and sea salt," Chef Bill explains. "If I'm eating an oyster and I can't have that, the experience just isn't the same."

To ensure the raw offerings are top-notch, Chef Bill sources them "as direct to the water as possible," using a local network to drop off and pick up from fishmongers and aquafarmers directly. "I'm looking for wild oysters of several kinds that are just out of the water," he explains. "Often, oysters are stored in sea water for up to a month before they are delivered! That's not happening on my watch." The rest of the shellfish — like shrimp, periwinkles, clams, and langoustines — are offered both raw and poached, gently cooked and cooled right before service. "You can taste the difference when shellfish has been treated better," Chef Bill says with a nod. "You can taste that level of care because the food is just full of flavor."

CHARCUTERIE AND CHEESE

The charcuterie program is new to La Grande Boucherie, an extension of the idea that no part of the animal should be wasted. Now that whole sides of pork and beef are brought into the restaurant to be processed in-house, the kitchen offerings of charcuterie have expanded significantly. Chef Bill has divided these into "dry" (cured, often whole cuts) and "fresh" (softer, stuffed, and cooked).

Hams (jambons) comprise an important part of the bar menu. As the rear legs of a pig make up almost a quarter of its full weight, they turn into an important family of meats, from jambon cuit (including jambon blanc, jambon a l'os, jambon au torchon, and jambonneau) to jambon sec (aged, dry hams, including jambon de bayonne, jamón serrano, and prosciutto). The next big category is sausages (saucissons), made with ground meat and stuffed into a casing (usually intestine). These are split into four categories: fresh and raw; air-dried or smoked (but still needing additional cooking); dried (typically salted, sometimes fermented to lower the pH); and cooked (a prominent example being mortadella). On La Grande Boucherie's menu, there are several sausage options, including saucissons a l'ail (pork and garlic) and saucissons sec (various dried sausages).

No charcuterie board would be complete without forcemeat, so there are options for both pâté (notably the pâté en croûte, which is set in flaky pastry dough) and terrines (like terrine de lapin, or rabbit terrine). There are also three different types of rillettes, where cuts of meat are cooked gently in their own fat and chilled under that fat shield for storage, similar to a duck confit.

For those more interested in cheese, the bar offers five: creamy, bloomy-rind Camembert; moist and salty goat milk Selles-sur-Cher, washed-rind, grassy Saint-Nectaire; classic, semi-hard Comté Vieux, and beautifully citrusy, tangy, sheep milk Fleur du Maquis. "There's something for everyone," explains owner Emil Stefkov about the philosophy of the cheese menu, "something to discover, or maybe something you love and want to have again." For those seeking pairings, Head Mixologist Milos Kostadinovic recommends guests "pick a wine from the same region, or surrounding region, of the cheese." Some tried-and-true duos include Sauvignon Blanc with goat cheese; juicy Bordeaux, red port, or dessert wine like Sauternes with blue cheese; and a Gewürztraminer from Alsace with buttery foie gras.

Finally, every piece of charcuterie or cheese is adorned with special accents like specialty almonds, herb-marinated olives, membrillo (quince paste), and fresh figs. Salty and sweet, crunchy, nutty, soft, even sticky — there are tastes and textures to complement and contrast every offering from the kitchen.

WINE AND COCKTAILS

The gallery outside La Grande Boucherie is
perpetually accessible, and the 18 trees that
adorn the space change with the seasons.
Fittingly, the indoor cocktail menu changes
as well. Head Mixologist Milos Kostadinovic
makes sure to capture the full array of New
York's seasons through his menu at all times.

In the summer, a wine glass of Le Mascaret — made of gin, rhubarb liqueur, Avèze (a French herbal liqueur made from gentian root), raspberry, and sparkling wine, garnished with a dehydrated dragonfruit wheel — is fitting for the hot weather. "It's named after the current that comes into the river from the ocean, creating a stream strong enough you can surf on it. In France, surfing these waves is called 'le mascaret.'" To nibble alongside, Milos suggests some lighter fare, like branzino or one of the salads. "It's a perfect afternoon: sipping this cocktail, eating some fresh vegetables, people-watching."

Milos has also dreamt up interesting variations on the classic French aperitif, Lillet. "There are three kinds of Lillet, which most people don't realize. There is white, red, and a rosé," he explains. The rosé variation is usually from the Cabernet Franc grape, and is excellent turned into a spritz with some sparkling wine and pink grapefruit. "That's always a favorite," Milos reports. "When it warms up in the city, I know I need to stock up on Lillet rosé."

As the temperature cools, the cocktail bar turns to an assortment of fruits, liqueurs, and spirits. Milos' newest creation is L'Envie ("desire" in French), his take on a margarita. It includes tequila blanco, grapefruit liqueur, mango puree, lime juice, and hellfire spicy bitters poured into a glass coated with absinthe and topped with a black salt rim. "The mango and the anise flavors pair well together," Milos explains, "and this reminds me of when I walk down the street in New York City and see the street vendors selling fresh sliced mangoes with a dusting of chile peppers."

L'ENVIE

"Desire" in French, our take on a classic Margarita.
Food pairing recommendation: pork chop, savory sauces

*"The mango and the anise flavors pair well together,
and this reminds me of when I walk down the street in
New York City and see the street vendors selling fresh
sliced mangoes with a dusting of chile peppers." –
Beverage Manager Milos Kostandinovic*

INGREDIENTS *Serves 1*

0.75oz mango puree
1oz fresh lime juice
0.25oz simple syrup
2oz tequila blanco
0.75oz pamplemousse liqueur
4 dashes hellfire spicy bitters

GARNISH

1oz absinthe vert
1 orange slice
Himalayan black salt, as needed
1 dehydrated lime wheel

PREPARATION

1. Add pebble ice in a rocks glass and pour in absinthe. Stir a few times and set aside.

2. In a cocktail shaker, add all ingredients over ice and shake vigorously.

3. Discard ice and absinthe from rock glass. Wet the rim of the glass with an orange slice, and add black salt to the rim.

4. Add fresh ice cubes into rock glass.

5. Strain and pour cocktail into glass.

6. Garnish with dehydrated lime wheel.

LE MASCARET

Summer cocktail made of gin, rhubarb liqueur, Avèze, and sparkling wine.
Food pairing recommendation: lighter fare, branzino or a salads.

"It's named after the current that comes into the river from the ocean, creating a stream strong enough you can surf on it. In France, surfing these waves is called 'le mascaret."– Beverage Manager Milos Kostandinovic

INGREDIENTS *Serves 1*

6 raspberries
0.5oz simple syrup
0.75oz lemon juice
1.5oz gin
0.5oz rhubarb liqueur
0.25oz Avèze
1oz sparkling wine

GARNISH

1 dehydrated dragonfruit wheel

PREPARATION

1. Combine all ingredients except sparkling wine with cold draft ice in cocktail shaker. Shake gently.

2. Pour cocktail through strainer into an 12oz all-purpose wine glass.

3. Top off cocktail with sparkling wine and garnish with dehydrated dragonfruit wheel.

BOUCHERIE